Viola Time Starters

a beginner book for viola

Kathy and David Blackwell

Illustrations by
Martin Remphry

MUSIC DEPARTMENT

OXFORD
UNIVERSITY PRESS

Great Clarendon Street, Oxford OX2 6DP, England

9 10

ISBN 978–0–19–336582–7

Music and text origination by Julia Bovee
Printed in Great Britain on acid-free paper by
Halstan & Co. Ltd, Amersham, Bucks.

Welcome to **Viola Time Starters**. You'll find:

- Lots of tunes to sing and then play
- A lively CD to listen and play along to
- Quizzes to do—grab a pencil
- 'Super listener' games—get your ears ready
- 'Be a composer' activities—get creative!

What you'll need:

Viola

Fingers and short fingernails

Rosin

Bow

Pencil

CD player

Got these? Let's get started.

Tune your strings to track 71–4 (A, D, G, C).

This book belongs to _____

Feel the beat

 Music has a steady beat, can you feel it in your feet?

 1 2 3 4 5 6 7 8

(*stamp feet*)

Hear the music in the band, can you feel it in your hands?

 1 2 3 4 5 6 7 8

(*clap hands*)

Now let's try a clever trick, can you make your fingers click?

 1 2 3 4 5 6 7 8

(*click fingers*)

'Feel the beat' is what I said, can you think it in your head?

 (1) (2) (3) (4) (5) (6) (7) **8**

(*count silently until beat eight*)

Music has a steady beat or pulse. Just like your heartbeat, it keeps going all the way through a song or tune. A fast tune will have a fast beat and a slower tune a slower beat.

Tap a steady beat and chant the words of a song you know well. Keep tapping all the way through.

3

Know your viola

Song time

Sing these words to the tune of 'Head, shoulders, knees, and toes' and point to the different parts of your instrument.

Scroll, shoulders, strings, and bridge, strings and bridge,
Scroll, shoulders, strings, and bridge, strings and bridge,
* And the pegs and chin-rest and the fingerboard,
Scroll, shoulders, strings, and bridge, strings and bridge.

* **Verse 2**: And the nut and *f* holes and the tail-piece,

Picture time

Draw a line from each word to the correct part of the viola.

scroll

pegs

nut

neck

bridge

shoulders

fingerboard

strings

f holes

chin-rest

adjusters

tail-piece

tail-button

Ready to play

Get-ready rag

Stand with your feet slightly apart and get ready to do each of the actions along with the CD. For 5–8, hold your viola steady with your right hand while you move to the music.

1. Rest position now,

2. Hold it out in front,

3. Lift it up on high,

4. On your shoulder now.

5. Feel the beat: sway on the spot, left and right.
6. Swinging hammock: swing your elbows.
7. High jump: tap your left hand on the strings or the wood either side of the fingerboard.
8. Long jump: slide your left hand up and down the fingerboard.

First sounds

In these tunes, pluck the open strings with your right-hand fingers. Make a big circle in the air with your right arm, like this:

4 Sway and strum

Sway gently from side to side in time to the music while you strum the strings.

| **1** | 2 | 3 | **1** | 2 | 3 |

Strum...   strum...   etc.

5 At the zoo

Listen to the sound of each string, then play the note pizzicato—that means plucking.

Listen

- A for alligators
- D for dolphins
- G for gorillas
- C for camels

Play and chant

- A for alligators
- D for dolphins
- G for gorillas
- C for camels

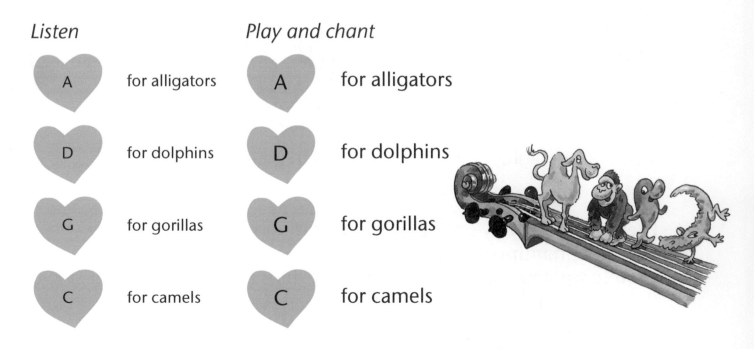

Chant
That's what we have in our zoo. Yeah!

Swing, swing, swing your arm

Sing and then play this piece to the tune of 'Row, row, row your boat'.

G   G   G   D

Swing,   swing,   swing your arm,   as we   sing this   song.

x2

G   G   D   G

Swing it out and   swing it in, we'll   swing it   all day   long.

Is your arm swinging away from each string?

 Flying around

C   A

Swing   with   your   arm   as   you

D   G

pluck   ev - 'ry   string.

C   A

Fly - ing   a - round   is   a

D   G

won - der - ful   thing!

Repeat once and end with a final C.

First tunes

Play these tunes pizzicato, placing your thumb on the edge of the fingerboard.

8 ## Counting beats

Play this piece four times, once with each string.

Chant
Counting beats is for the best, play four Cs* then count four rests.

Play   x4

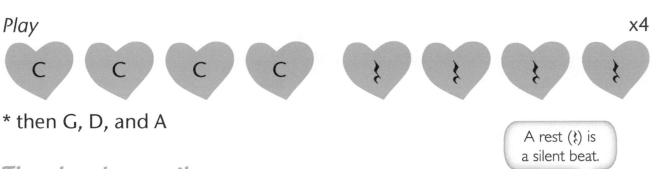

* then G, D, and A

> A rest (𝄽) is a silent beat.

9 ## The drunken sailor

Sing
Let's all play pizzicato, let's all play pizzicato,
Let's all play pizzicato, early in the morning.

Play

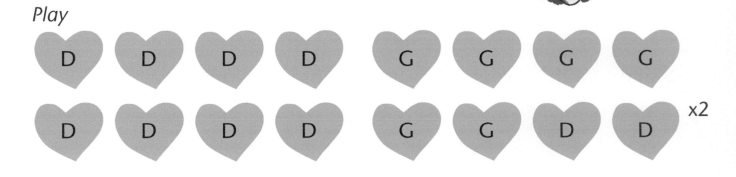

10 ## Jelly on a plate

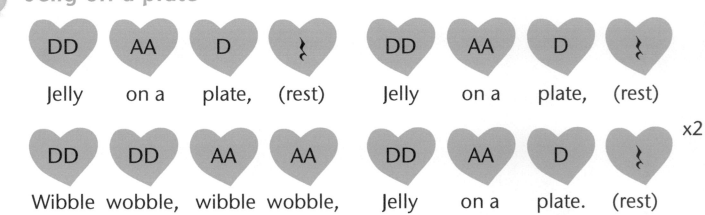

Super listener

When you can sing and then play 'Jelly on a plate' really well, try a lower version starting on the G string. Then play an even lower version—which string will you begin on?

Be a composer

1. Make up your own tune by playing the pattern of the following words on your open strings. Tap a steady beat and say the words through a few times before you start.

'I hear footsteps on the street.
Someone's there with great big feet!'

2. Invent your own tune using notes from the boxes. Write your tune in the heartbeat spaces—one box per heartbeat—and then play it from start to finish.

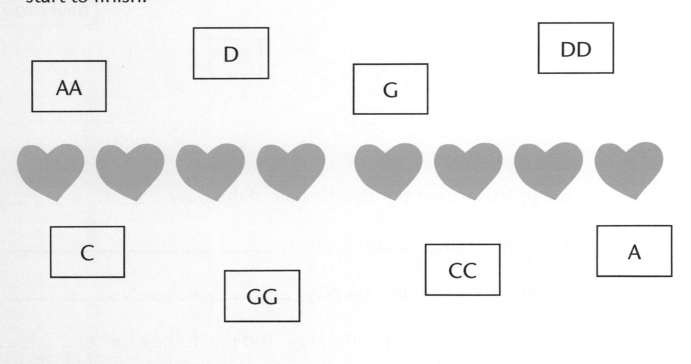

Give your tune a title: _____

Know your bow

 ## Song time

Sing these words along with the CD and point to the different parts of the bow.

1. There's the point and the heel and the stick in between,
   Don't touch the hair to keep it clean.

2. Turn the screw to the right to make the hair tight,
   Rosin the bow and off we go.

3. Turn the screw to the left to loosen the bow,
   That's what we do when it's time to go.

Picture time

Draw a line from each word to the correct part of the bow.

stick

point (tip)

screw

heel (frog)

hair

Quiz time

What am I?

You turn me to loosen and tighten the hair of the bow: _____

I'm part of the bow that you don't touch: _____

You rub me on the hair before you play: _____

You'll find the heel at one end of the bow and me at the other end: _____

Yo bow!

Get ready to perform this bow-hold rap by holding the middle of the stick with your left hand. The tip of the bow will point to your left.

1. Shake your right hand to the ground,
   Wiggle those fingers all around.

2. Hang your fingers right over the stick,
   Slightly apart now, that's the trick.

3. Lean your hand, don't let it drop,
   Put your little finger right on top.

4. Bend your thumb and bring it round,
   Keep it curved to make a great sound.

5. Yo bow! Yo bow!
   To the left, to the right, and off we go.

6. Yo bow! Yo bow!
   Up and down and off we go.

Have you got a smiley thumb? Look through the round hole made by your thumb and middle fingers.

7. Yo bow! Yo bow!
   Round and round and off we go.

8. Yo bow! Yo bow!
   Side to side and off we go.

Down- and up-bow signs

⊓ This is a down-bow sign—pull your right hand away from the strings.
V This is an up-bow sign—push your right hand up towards the strings.

Play this pattern on each open string: ⊓   V   ⊓   V
                                          down   up down   up

Move the bow up and down, keeping it parallel to the bridge.

Following the signs

Choose one of these patterns and play it a few times on an open string.

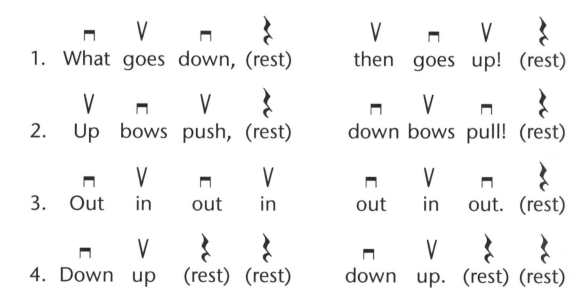

1. ⊓ What   V goes   ⊓ down,   𝄽 (rest)   V then   ⊓ goes   V up!   𝄽 (rest)

2. V Up   ⊓ bows   V push,   𝄽 (rest)   ⊓ down   V bows   ⊓ pull!   𝄽 (rest)

3. ⊓ Out   V in   ⊓ out   V in   ⊓ out   V in   ⊓ out.   𝄽 (rest)

4. ⊓ Down   V up   𝄽 (rest)   𝄽 (rest)   ⊓ down   V up.   𝄽 (rest)   𝄽 (rest)

Try the same patterns on your rosin. Make sure the bow moves and not the rosin!

Now play the tunes on page 8 arco—that means with the bow. For 'The drunken sailor', change the words to 'Let's all play arco'.

'walk'
crotchet (or quarter-note)

'jogging'
quavers (or eighth-notes)

- Clap the rhythms below, saying 'walk' for each ♩ and 'jogging' for each ♫
- Ask someone to tap the beat while you clap the rhythms, and then swap.
- Choose one row of beats (a bar or measure) and play that rhythm on each open string. For Set 1, count a steady **1**-2-3-4, **1**-2-3-4 before you start. For Set 2, count **1**-2-3, **1**-2-3.
- Finally, play each ♩ on the G string and each ♫ on the D string, or choose two other strings that are next to each other.

$\frac{4}{4}$ is a **time signature**. It means four ♩ beats in each bar.

What do you think $\frac{3}{4}$ means?

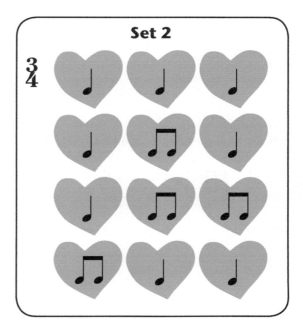

13 **Super listener**

Listen to track 13, 'Echo calypso', and copy back the rhythms on the D and A strings.

Open-string rap

Chant

Viola strings from high to low, let me tell you how they go.
First there's A then D then G, way down low you'll find the C.
A D G C. Way down low you'll find the C.

Play each string from high to low, start with A and down you go.

Chant

Play each string from low to high, start with C then reach for the sky!

Quiz time

Draw the correct open string above each letter to spell the words as notes.

What words do these notes spell? Fill in the name of each string to find out.

Walk and jogging tunes

At the zoo

This is a barline:
It divides music into bars.

A double barline comes at the end of a tune:

Be a composer

Make up your own rhythms using the open strings. Think of something beginning with each letter and then play the pattern of the words on each string. You could use the names of friends or different places as starting points. Write your words in the spaces below:

A for _____

D for _____

G for _____

C for _____

16 Copycat blues

When the music repeats, the rhythm is different—it sounds like 'We are the champions!'. Listen carefully and copy what you hear.

17 Mini Mozart

This is a repeat sign:

Mozart, arr. KB/DB

Mo - zart,   Mo - zart,   etc.

Try these rhythm variations:

etc.

Wolf-gang A - ma - de - us,   Wolf-gang A - ma - de - us,

etc.

Walk   jog - ging walk,   walk   jog - ging walk,

etc.

Pull   to   the   tip then   push   to   the   heel then

18 Boogie band

With energy

Boo-gie on the o-pen D, boo-gie on the o-pen G, boo-gie on the o-pen D,

boo-gie on the A. Boo-gie on the o-pen D, boo-gie on the o-pen G,

Shout

boo-gie on the D then G. Yeah!

19 Rhythm train

Verse 1

Lively

Listen *Copy* (etc.)

O-ver-night ex-press train, O-ver-night ex-press train, etc.

Verse 2

Listen *Copy* etc.

All a-board, all a-board, All a-board, all a-board,

End with some train whistle sounds!

Verse 3

Listen *Copy* etc.

Train whis-tle, train whis-tle, Train whis-tle, train whis-tle,

20 Super listener

Listen to track 20 and play 'Rhythm train' using your C and G strings.

21 ## Mr Pizzicato and friends

Sing the words and play the notes in each verse.

Verse 1

Mr Pizzicato likes to pluck the string, he puts his finger here and he lets it ring:

Mr Pizzicato likes to pluck the string.

Verse 2

Mr Arco has a great bow-hold, he strokes the strings and it sounds so bold:

Mr Arco has a great bow-hold.

Verse 3

Mr Col Legno likes to use the wood, he bounces very gently and it sounds real good:

Mr Col Legno likes to use the wood.

Verse 4

Mr Tremolo likes to shiver with his bow, so he puts it near the tip and this is how it goes:

Mr Tremolo likes to shiver with his bow.

End the song with tremolo on the D string.

Use your new tremolo skills to play a spooky version of 'The drunken sailor' on page 8. Change the words to 'Let's all play with tremolo bowing'.

String-crossing tunes

In these string-crossing tunes, watch your elbow swing *up* when you play a lower string and *down* when you play a higher string.

22 **Happy Haydn**

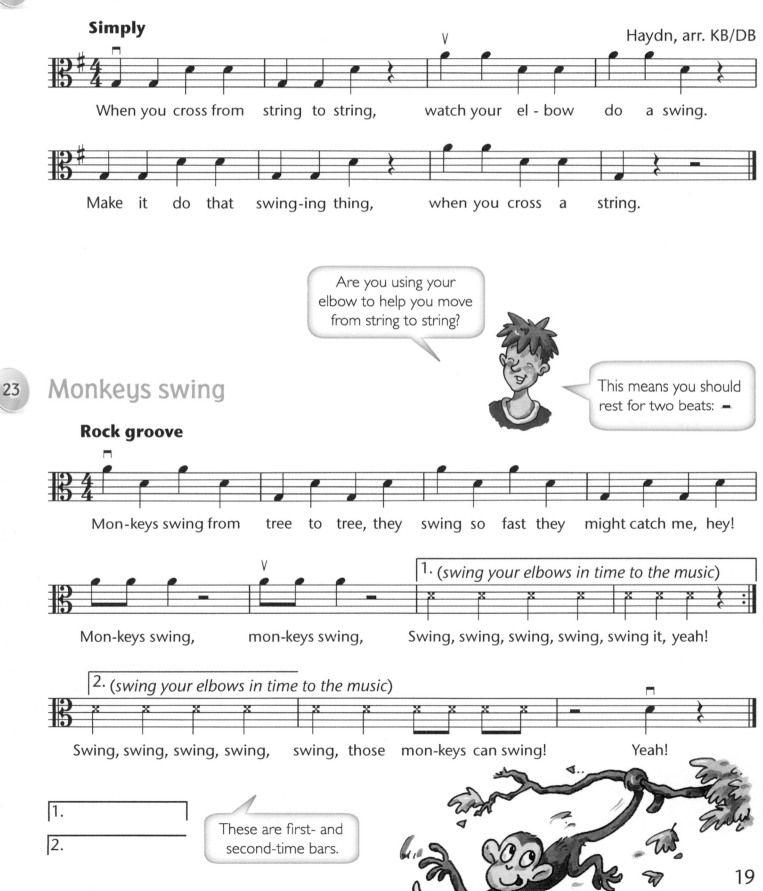

23 **Monkeys swing**

Rhythm zone 2: slow-walk

Say and clap the rhythm below while a friend or teacher taps the beat, and then swap over. Remember to count and feel two beats for each ♩

'slow - walk'
minim (or half-note)

Walk walk walk walk, slow - walk slow-walk, etc.

24 ## Classical sounds

Verse 1

Gracefully

Walk walk slow-walk, walk walk slow-walk, etc.

Verse 2

Slow-walk walk walk, slow-walk walk walk,

Verse 3

At the heel then slow-walk, at the tip then slow-walk,

25 ## Super listener

Listen to track 25 and play 'Classical sounds' using your D and G strings. The first note will be open D.

Slow-walk tunes

26 **Raindrops**

27 **Swing band**

Left-hand pizzicato

In these tunes you'll need to use left-hand pizzicato. When you see the **+** sign, pluck the string with your left-hand 4th finger.

28 **Chinese festival**

29 **Popcorn**

First sing the song and play left-hand pizzicato in the 'Pop! Bang!' bars. Then play with right-hand pizzicato or arco for the rest of the tune, but keep using your left hand for 'Pop! Bang!'.

Finger jogging time

Four joggers

Say this rhyme and tap each fingertip in turn on your left-hand thumb.

	Four	jog-gers	out	one	day,	one	fell	down	and	lost	his	way.
4th finger:	Four	jog-gers	out	one	day,	one	fell	down	and	lost	his	way.
3rd finger:	Three	jog-gers	out	one	day,	one	fell	down	and	lost	his	way.
2nd finger:	Two	jog-gers	out	one	day,	one	fell	down	and	lost	his	way.
1st finger:	One	jog-ger	out	one	day,	he	fell	down	and	lost	his	way.
0 fingers:	No	jog-gers	out	to-day!		(Stop!)						

30 Super listener

Listen to track 30 and play 'Four joggers' on your A string, starting with your 4th finger and lifting a finger off between each line.

Sporty rhythms

Shape up your left-hand fingers on the D string. Choose a sporty rhythm from below and play it on each fingered note and on the open D: 4–32–1–0. Make sure that your 2nd and 3rd fingers are close together.

Walk   walk   slow - walk,

Jog-ging walk   jog-ging walk,

Rea - dy, stea - dy, go   now,

Quick   run - ner, fast   sprint-er,

Also try playing up the notes from the open string: 0–1–23–4.

Finger jogging tunes

You can play these tunes on any string, but if you play with the CD, make sure you use the string shown.

31 ## Fingers and feet (D string)

$\frac{4}{4}$

22	22	33	33	22	22	11	11
From our	fingers	to our	feet, we	always	keep a	steady	beat, we

22	22	33	33	22	11	0	
keep it	going	in a	song if	notes are	short or	long_____.	

(Stamp feet eight times, then repeat.)

32 ## Roller coaster (D string)

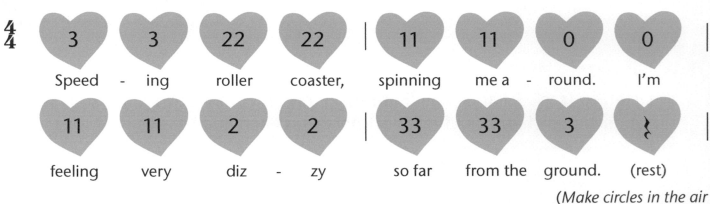

$\frac{4}{4}$

3	3	22	22	11	11	0	0
Speed	- ing	roller	coaster,	spinning	me a -	round.	I'm

11	11	2	2	33	33	3	𝄽
feeling	very	diz	- zy	so far	from the	ground.	(rest)

(Make circles in the air with the bow, then repeat.)

33 ## String band (A string)

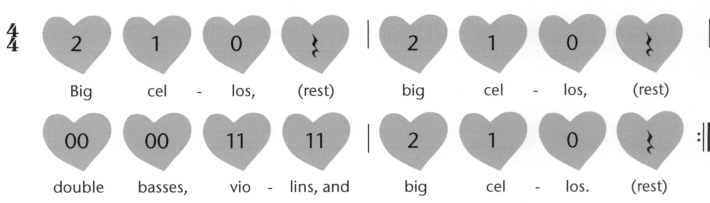

$\frac{4}{4}$

2	1	0	𝄽	2	1	0	𝄽
Big	cel	- los,	(rest)	big	cel	- los,	(rest)

00	00	11	11	2	1	0	𝄽
double	basses,	vio	- lins, and	big	cel	- los.	(rest)

Can an imaginary mouse run in a straight line from the tip of your elbow to your knuckles?

(34) Rain, rain (A string)

4/4	3	1	33	1		33	11	33	1
	Rain,	rain,	go a	- way,		please don't	rain on	Satur	- day.

(35) Twinkle, twinkle, little star

This tune uses two different strings—a lower one and a higher one. CD track 35 is played on the D and A strings.

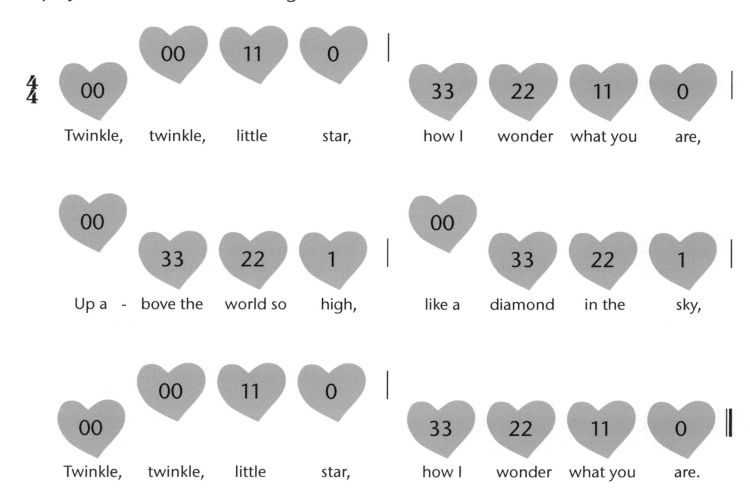

4/4	00	00	11	0		33	22	11	0
	Twinkle,	twinkle,	little	star,		how I	wonder	what you	are,

00	33	22	1		00	33	22	1
Up a	- bove the	world so	high,		like a	diamond	in the	sky,

00	00	11	0		33	22	11	0
Twinkle,	twinkle,	little	star,		how I	wonder	what you	are.

(36) Super listener

Listen to track 36 and play 'Twinkle, twinkle, little star' starting on the G string.

Be a composer

Using the words below, make up your own tune using the left-hand fingers. Tap a steady beat and say the words through a few times before you start.

'Deep in the jungle, what do you see?
Alligators, alligators after me!'

D-string notes

1st finger makes the note E

2nd finger makes the note F#

3rd finger makes the note G

This is a sharp sign: #

37 This is G

This is G, G G G, ev-'ry-bo-dy rea-dy with a G G G.

38 Jogging in the city

Hold your 3rd finger down and be sure to leave an 'A-string tunnel'.

Jog - ging in the ci - ty, jog - ging down the street. We're

off to jog in Lon - don, al - ways to the beat.

39 Perfect match

1. Oc - taves are sounds that are eight notes a - part.
2. Tune your 3rd fin - ger with your o - pen G.

Play them each day, it's a great way to start.
Play it and make those Gs match per - fect - ly.

The sharps at the start of the music are called **key signatures**.

40 F sharp now

F sharp now,   show me how,   ev-'ry-bo-dy rea-dy with an   F sharp now.

41 Venice and Vivaldi

Vivaldi, arr. KB/DB

Ve - nice and Vi - val - di,

Ve - nice and Vi - val - di,   Ve - nice and Vi - val - di.

42 Here comes E

Here comes E,   E   E   E,   ev-'ry-bo-dy rea-dy with an   E   E   E.

43 Starlight

Star - light,   star   bright,   if   I   close   my   eyes   tight,

if   I   wish   with   all   my   might,   can   I   have   my   wish   to - night?

44 Super listener

Play 'Starlight' using the open A string and F♯ on the D string. Hold your 2nd finger down all the way through and let your open A string ring out clearly.

Star - light,   star   bright,

D-string activity page

Writing time

Draw these D-string notes on the stave below:

Bar 1: ♩ x 4 on open D

Bar 2: 𝅗𝅥 x 2 on E

Bar 3: ♩ 𝄽 ♩ 𝄽 on F#

Bar 4: 𝅗𝅥 on G and a two-beat rest

Now draw a down-bow sign above the first note and play the tune through.

Roller coaster quiz

Play 'Roller coaster' on page 24 and then do the quiz below.

Speed - ing   rol - ler   coast - er,   spin - ning   me   a - round.   I'm

feel - ing   ve - ry   diz - zy   so   far   from   the ground.

• Some notes are missing in the tune. Fill them in where you see the * sign.

• Draw a circle around the time signature.

• Fill in the missing number: 𝄴 means _____ ♩ beats in a bar.

• A ♩ rest is missing in bar 4. Draw it in correctly.

• Draw a circle around some ♫ Es.

• How many F#s can you count in the first line? _____

D-string tunes

45 ## Fit as a fiddle

Play the rhythm variations in verses 2 and 3 and end each verse with the chorus.

Verse 1

Doh comes first to start the show, ray comes next and up we go,
D comes first to start the show, E comes next and up we go,

mi comes now, I'll show you how, then fa fa fa fa soh soh!
F sharp now, I'll show you how, then G G G G A A!

Chorus

Doh ray mi fa soh soh soh soh doh.
D E F# G A A A A D.

Verse 2

Walk jog-ging jog-ging walk,   etc.

Verse 3

Walk walk (rest) walk,   etc.

46 ## Finger-tapping cha-cha

Fin - ger - tap - ping cha - cha, fin - ger - tap - ping cha - cha,

feel the cha-cha rhy - thm down to your toes. Fin-ger-tap-ping cha - cha,

fin-ger-tap-ping cha - cha, feel the cha-cha rhy - thm, that's how it goes.

Chant this as you tap your left-hand 3rd finger on the string:

Tap your finger, wiggle your thumb. Tap your finger, wiggle your thumb. Tap your finger, wiggle your thumb. Let's get ready, now here it comes. (*repeat the piece*)

Lost shoe blues

Play with a swing

G I'm blue, lost my shoe, don't know where I put it, got the

lost shoe blues. I'll miss the bus, what a fuss!

late for school and teach-er's mad, I feel so sad. I'll have to hop,

and not stop, don't know where I put it, got the lost shoe blues.

The next piece is in **2/4**.
What do you think that means?

Missed it!

On the move

Run-ning to the rail - way sta - tion, hope the train will be on time. I've

checked the time and des - tin - a - tion, it's on plat-form nine. Oh!

Train went past, it left with-out me, sped right down that rail - way line. I'm

stand-ing here at plat-form one, not plat-form num-ber nine!

At the end of the piece, slide your left hand up and down the fingerboard like a fast train.

A-string notes

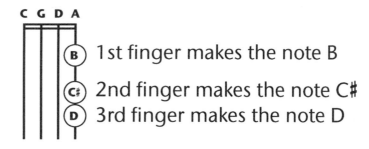

B) 1st finger makes the note B

C#) 2nd finger makes the note C#

D) 3rd finger makes the note D

49 **This is D**

This is D,   D   D   D,   ev-'ry-bo-dy rea-dy with a   D   D   D.

50 **Super listener**

Play 'Perfect match' on page 26 starting on your open D string.

51 **C sharp now**

C sharp now,   show me how,   ev-'ry-bo-dy rea-dy with a   C sharp now.

52 **Knock, knock!**

Knock, knock! Who's there?   Frank - ie.   Frank-ie who?   Frank-ly,   it's   none of your

busi - ness!

Think of your favourite 'Knock, knock'
jokes and play them using these notes.

53 Here comes B

Here comes B, B B B, ev-'ry-bo-dy rea-dy with a B B B.

54 Off to school

On the go

Friends and I, we walk to school, we walk walk walk walk, that's our rule. Walk walk walk walk walk walk walk.

Then when it's time to go home from school, we're jog-ging jog-ging jog-ging jog-ging, that's our rule! Jog-ging jog-ging jog-ging jog-ging. Phew let's stop!

Slower l.h. pizz.

* Tap your 3rd finger on the A string.

55 Wake up!

Insistent

Wake up in the morn - in', got - ta stop your snor - in',

wake up in the morn - in', wake up! Here's your fi - nal warn - in',

got - ta stop your yawn - in', here's your fi - nal warn - in', get up!

A-string activity page

Writing time

Draw the A-string notes on the stave below. Each note will be a ♩

A   B   C#   D

Be an A-string composer

Use the rhythm shown to write your own tune using the A-string notes. Choose one note per bar.

Ice   skat - ing,   ice   skat - ing,   quick   as   can   be.

Slip - ping   and   slid - ing, oops!   fell   on   my   knee!

Now draw a down-bow sign above the first note and play your tune through.

56 **Get aboard**

Try some swinging rhythms in verses 2 and 3. Listen to track 56 to hear how it goes and get the swing of it!

Verse 1

Swinging along

Get a-board the rhy-thm train, we're head-ing out of town, yeah.

Get a-board the rhy-thm train for we're Chi-ca-go bound.

Verse 2

Chickety-can, it goes speeding along, it goes
Chickety-can, it goes speeding along, it goes
Chickety-can, it goes speeding along, it goes
Chickety-can all day long!

Verse 3

Speeding here and speeding there, it
Speeds right down the railway track, it's
Speeding here and speeding there, don't
Know when we'll be back!

57 **Clear blue sky**

Gently

1. Come and fly, way up high, we will see clear blue sky.
2. Like a bird fly-ing round, soar-ing far from the ground.
3. Fly-ing high on the wing, see them swoop, hear them sing.

34

Harmonic-ky things

Octave harmonics: to find this special sound, touch the string very lightly about halfway along with your 4th finger. This is the harmonic sign: ○

58 Harmonic-ky thing

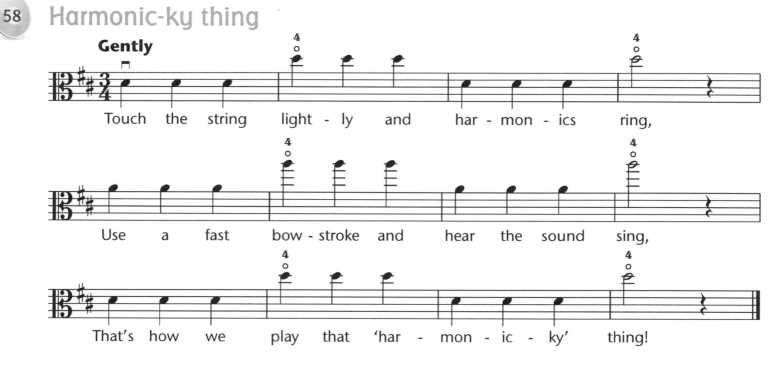

Touch the string light - ly and har - mon - ics ring,

Use a fast bow - stroke and hear the sound sing,

That's how we play that 'har - mon - ic - ky' thing!

59 Emma's lullaby

Em-ma's lul-la-by, lie still, close your eyes, Em-ma's lul-la-by, sleep now.

Can you find the octave harmonic on the C string?

Clear blue sky

Play this harmonic part while your friend or teacher plays the tune on the opposite page, then swap over. Use track 57 on the CD.

1. Come and fly, way up high, we will see clear blue sky.
2. Like a bird fly - ing round, soar - ing far from the ground.
3. Fly - ing high on the wing, see them swoop, hear them sing.

Scale-y things

60 Scale builder

Listen ... *Copy*

Can you play the D-string notes and co-py me? Doh ray mi fa. Doh ray mi fa.
D E F# G. D E F# G.

Listen ... *Copy*

Now play the A string, but lis-ten first to me: Soh la ti doh. Soh la ti doh.
A B C# D. A B C# D.

Listen ... *Play together*

Can you play the scale of D a-long with me? Doh ray mi fa soh la ti doh.
D E F# G A B C# D.

Listen ... *Play together*

Let's play the whole scale to-ge-ther, you and me: Doh ray mi fa soh la ti doh.
D E F# G A B C# D.

Listen ... *Play together*

We have played a scale to-ge-ther now. That's it!

Scale-y dragon

Choose an idea from the scale-y dragon and play a scale of D major in that way. Make up some more ideas of your own.

Make your own rhythm and play it on each note.

PLAY quietly.

Play each note three times.

Play each note twice.

Play pizzicato.

Play as a round with a friend.

Play an insect rhythm on each note.

Sing the scale UP and down.

Scale of D major

Play a different rhythm for each note of the scale.

Play ⁴₄ rhythms with track 61 . Play ³₄ rhythms with track 62 .

63 Aiming high

Confidently

With each sound the notes go high - er, climb-ing up, we're all high fli - ers,

aim-ing high, we'll ne - ver ev - er stop un - til we reach the top!

Play 'Aiming high' as a round. The second part enters at *.

Super listener

Play a scale starting on your G or C string.

64 G major ³₄   65 C major ⁴₄

Play with your eyes shut!

Play **LOUDLY**

Play the rhythm of your name on each note

Play a foody rhythm on each note, e.g. 'I like bananas.'

Play from top to bottom.

Show tunes

66 Souallé

Like a lullaby

Lul - la - by,   sweet dreams to-night,   etc.

Slower (2nd time only)

(**1**   2   3,   **1**   2   3,   **1**   2   3)

67 Snap!

Creepy

arco

Sca - ly   skin,   ra - zor   teeth,   prowl - ing   for   his   lunch,

Look - ing   for   some-thing sweet,   some-thing   he   can crunch.

If   he   comes   creep - ing   near,   don't   be   too   po - lite,

Fine

Cro - co - diles   al - ways smile,   but   they   like   to   bite.

D.C. al Fine

pizz.

Snap, snap, snap!   Snap, snap, snap!   Snap, snap, snap!   Snap, snap, snap!

D.C. al Fine means repeat from the start and stop at the word **Fine**.

68 More Mini Mozart

Gracefully

Mo - zart wrote mu - sic he played on the pia - no, he

wrote lots of tunes and he played all day long.

Try these rhythm variations:

Walk jog-ging walk, walk jog-ging walk,

Walk jog-ging jog-ging, walk jog-ging jog-ging,

69 Hide and seek

On the move

Run - ning round the play - ground, look - ing for my friends, I

just can't find them here, it's hide and seek a-gain, I think that I spy some-one

hid-ing o - ver there, but oops there goes the bell, it's just not fair!

Happily

Sum - mer's here, the sun is shin-ing bright - ly, time to have a ho - li -

- day. Blue skies, blue sea, sand be-tween my toes, and

ice-cream on the beach to - day! Sum - mer's here, the

sun is shin-ing bright - ly, I just love the ho - li - days, yes I do!